What is Facilities Management All About

"...the practice of facilities management for today's dynamic business environment."

Steven Ee

Copyright © 2018 Steven Ee

All rights reserved. No portion of this book may be reproduced or transmitted in any form or by any means — photocopy, scanning, or otherwise, without the prior permission of the author, except for inclusion of brief quotations in reviews or articles.

What is Facilities Management All About?

. . . the practice of facilities management for today's dynamic business environment.

Author: Steven Ee
Website: www.stevenee.com
Email: steven@stevenee.com
ISBN-13: 978-1986717038
ISBN-10: 1986717038

CONTENT

INTRODUCTION I

1 THE MISSION OF FACILITIES MANAGEMENT 1
    WHY DOES FM EXIST IN AN ORGANIZATION? 3
    WHAT VALUES ARE ORGANIZATIONS LOOKING FOR IN FM? 5
    THE PRACTICE OF FM - FACILITATES OPERATIONS SUCCESS 10

2 WHY FM SHOULD BE A STRATEGIC FUNCTION. 15
    FM PROFESSIONAL IDENTITY 16
    WHY IS IT IMPORTANT TO DEFINE THE PROFESSIONAL IDENTITY OF FM? 17
    WHY IS IT SO DIFFICULT TO DEFINE THE PROFESSIONAL IDENTITY OF FM? 18
    CASE FOR FM AS A STRATEGIC FUNCTION 23

3 WHY FM IS NOT A COST CENTRE 33
    SO, WHY IS FM NOT A COST CENTER? 34
    WORTH OF FM VALUE CONTRIBUTIONS 38
    FM AS A BUSINESS ADVANTAGE TO ORGANIZATIONS 40

4 GETTING STARTED 43

CONCLUSION 57

RESOURCES 59

REFERENCE 60

INTRODUCTION

"What is Facilities Management?" is designed for new or even seasoned practitioners in facilities management (FM) who are feeling frustrated working in FM, for those who are facing difficulty in articulating the value of FM as a business resource to their senior management and stakeholders, and those who are looking for a clear path in advancing their FM career. It is also meant for those who are tired of begging for their FM budget or tackling capital improvements with a handful of pennies.

For many years, senior management have perceived FM as an order taking function, a cost center, a support role and a non-strategic function. Due to these, FM practitioners are not usually involved in the decision making process of their organizations. Because FM practitioners don't get involved at the strategic level, their functions are always directed by other services in the organizations.

Apart from being isolated from the core business decision-making processes of their organization, FM practitioners are often out of synch with the core business strategies of their various organizations. Not to mention that they are often unable to advance their roles as strategic partners.

As mentioned earlier, many FM practitioners feel frustrated working in FM because of the above perceptions of FM. So, this book is timely to help FM practitioners to articulate and elevate the value of their functions to senior management.

The above senior management perceptions of FM were formed at a time when FM hadn't evolved so much. Today, businesses expect their facilities to be employee-centric, reinforces their corporate brand; adapts to support the new work-life models, and drive staff productivity. Consequently, FM practitioners have a more significant opportunity to elevate their functions to strategic ones in their organizations now more than before.

Book Objectives

To help readers to:

- Appreciate the mission of FM as a function within an organization, its critical activities and the expected performance outcome of FM services

- Understand that for FM to be able to keep pace with organizational strategic objectives and to facilitate their success, FM needs to operate from a strategic level;

- FM operations are to sustain and contribute to the wealth of its organization;

- Get started to practice right FM right.

Let's dive in!

1

THE MISSION OF FACILITIES MANAGEMENT

Let's start by clarifying and understanding the Mission of FM. The word "Mission" refers to an important task assigned to someone or a team. Once a person or group understands their mission, it provides clarity and direction in executing the mission.

So, to execute a function properly, the mission of that function must be clearly understood.

For instance, if someone sends you to the grocery store to get some supplies, your mission is obvious, and once you get to the grocery store, you get your supplies and leave. But if you don't understand your mission to the store, you could get there and do something entirely different from what you were sent to do. So, to execute a function properly, the mission must be clearly understood.

That explains why we want to start this book by talking about the mission of FM. When you understand the mission of FM, you are motivated to know the activities and their tasks you are supposed to perform to reach this mission.

The mission of FM provides direction and focus for the FM team, on what FM needs to accomplish.

That being said, what is the "Mission of FM?" Were you caught off guard by this question? Well, you are not alone. In fact, many people, whom I've asked, were caught off guard when asked, even those seasoned FM practitioners often find it difficult to precisely define their mission; so you are not alone.

To understand the mission of FM, let us look at two important questions; the answers to these two essential questions will help you understand the mission of FM. First, why does FM exist in an organization? Second, what values are organizations looking for in FM?

Why does FM exist in an organization?

FM exists to manage the non-core activities that support an organization's core business activities. In every organization, there are always the core and non-core activities. If your organization is an IT company, for instance, that is charged with developing software programs and enterprise applications for businesses, the core activities of your organization becomes to write software codes, to arrange business analysis meetings, and to train clients on how to use their new solutions.

FM exists to manage the non-core activities that support an organization's core business activities.

So, what are the non-core activities? Well, they are mainly the building and support services. Example, non-core activities could include things such as:

- making sure that the lights works
- making sure that the air conditioning is comfort-able
- making sure that waste is collected
- making sure that workspaces are clean

- overseeing the security systems and ensuring the office premises are safe for people to use

What do we mean by the non-core activities that support an organization's core business activities? For instance, the air conditioning and mechanical ventilation (ACMV) system in an organization. The functions or operations that make them work well, are not the core functions of the organization. However, when the ACMV system is working well – i.e. clean air, at a comfortable temperature level and ventilation, is circulating within the building or facilities of the organization. The effect is that workers don't fall sick easily due to poor air quality. When workers are healthy, business operation is continued and the productivity is improved.

Also, if the ACMV fails, the working conditions for the workers may become unbearable and affect their work performance. In some industry like data center, it will disrupt the business' operations and impact the revenues.

What values are organizations looking for in FM?

Do you think that your organization is satisfied with FM just managing the non-core activities? Will a smooth running operations impress the top management or it is expected? Will the management be impressed that you managed to resuscitate the 15-year-old chiller? What qualities will make your FM stands out?

Below are some of the organisation's expectation from today's in-demand FM services.

i. Safety and health

FM services always ensure that members of the public, employees, and visitors to the organization are as safe as possible in accordance with the mandatory required health and safety work procedures. FM services are expected to handle on-site emergencies to ensure that everyone in the organization is safe from accidents and other hazards. A safe and healthy working environment will also increase staff's morale and retention.

ii. Security

The provision of intruder alarm systems, security safeguarding systems and other security guarding services also help to ensure that the organization's building and its other properties are safe from the activities of an intruder, vandalism, and protection to the occupants at all time.

iii. Compliance with legal requirements and organization's policy

There are a lot of legal requirements that organizations are to comply with and non-compliance with these regulations attracts many sanctions. Many of these requirements usually border around the safety of the workplace, the security and the general welfare of people in the workplace and environment protection. Ensuring that organizations comply with these many legal requirements often lies on the shoulder of FM.

Safety and health requirements are among the major requirements or regulations that organizations are meant to comply with.

However, there are many others, including:

- Contract law
- Employment law
- Environmental legislation
- Waste regulations

As said earlier, the consequences for not complying with these various regulations can be severe. Regulatory bodies can fine organizations enormous sums for non-compliance, not to mention that organizations can experience expensive business downtime due to shut down order and suffer from loss of reputation due to bad press and the loss of effective working duration due to investigation by the regulatory bodies.

iv. Pleasant customer experience

When the organization's facilities and buildings are clean, secure and safe for not just the employees but also to the general public, customers enjoy pleasant experiences and would want to continue dealing with the organization. When the customers experience care, respect, and their health and safety are considered within the organization's facility, they are likely to continue patronizing the organization. So, a major expectation of FM services is the provision of pleasant experiences to customers.

v. Optimizing resources and reducing costs

Apart from the employment of staff, FM services account for some of the most substantial costs to an organization. So, another expectation of FM is the reduction of its operations costs. FM that can be creative in the use of office space, improved energy efficiency and increased productivity often will impress the top management.

vi. Corporate Social Responsibility

In layman's words, Corporate Social Responsibility (CSR) is how an organization gives back to its host community and the wider world in a positive way. CSR is good for organizations; it portrays organizations in a positive light to the wider world and promotes brand loyalty.

FM potential contributions toward CSR include environmental protection initiatives and supporting the organisation's CSR schemes such as continual improvement to the working lives of employees, etc.

vii. **Maintenance of business continuity**

Business continuity is achieved when an organization is able to continue their operations even in the face of crisis. Crisis can come in many forms ranging from a full-scale natural disaster to a simple power outage.

Business continuity is critical for any business, as downtime can lead to:

- Disgruntled customers
- Loss of reputation
- Loss of revenue

Business continuity in mission-critical organizations can be the difference between life and death. FM contribution towards business continuity by being prepared for emergencies.

In the event of disaster, FM is to support in the disaster recovery, relating to restoring the facilities services and providing support services, to enable the organization to restore to business as usual state at the soonest time possible.

The practice of FM - facilitates operations success

It is what in-demand FM all about. It is not only to provide the facilities operation and maintenance; it helps facilitate the organization's operations success. Let us look at it more deeply so that you may understand better.

To facilitate means "to make some-thing possible or easier." "To facilitate an organization's operations success" will mean that FM's efforts are intended and directed to contribute to the success of an organization's operations.

To facilitate an organization's operations success will mean that FM's efforts are intended and directed to contribute to the success of an organization's operations.

For example, in the case of increasing trend of remote working, introducing hot desking and hoteling, will helps the organization to control costs through the efficient management of facilities. Implementing flexible designed workstations system creates a fast-paced, collaborative and productive environment.

The FM team will be expected to enable the organization to keep pace and adapt to the dynamic change of the business environment – the speed of adaptability is crucial to the survival and success of the business.

Thus the mission of FM is not just to support the business operation but facilitate its operations success.

Now, to be able to facilitate the success of your organization's operations, it is vital that you know your organization's business operations, such as their processes and activities in producing the products or services for its customers.

The understanding of these business operations will

enable you to appreciate the importance of the facilities, identify the critical facilities services that enable the effectiveness and efficiency of the organization's business activities, which will, in turn, help you to prioritize your decisions and resources allocation.

> *FM practice should be to maximize the performance of physical assets, contribute to the organization's operational efficiency, and protect the company's profitability.*

The bottom line is that the mission for today's in-demand FM practice should be to maximize the performance of physical assets, contribute to the organization's operational efficiency, and protect the company's profitability. However, you are unlikely to appreciate your organization's business operations, the core processes and their activities unless you are operating FM functions at a strategic level. I hope this reason explains why you need to impress upon the senior management of your organization to re-cognize FM as a strategic function. If FM is not recognized, thus, not operating as a strategic function, you will remain at the mercy of other functions to get the things you need such as the funds required to run your department. Your services are then often reactive instead of proactive.

The bottom line is that the mission for today's in-demand FM practice should be to maximize the performance of the physical assets, contribute to the organization's operational efficiency, and protect the company's profitability.

2

WHY FM SHOULD BE A STRATEGIC FUNCTION

Having laid a good foundation in the previous chapter, we can see why FM should be a strategic function. For FM to be able to keep pace with organizational strategic objectives and facilitate their success, FM should be a strategic function and the duty of making FM a strategic function rests on the shoulders of every FM practitioner.

For FM to be able to keep pace with organizational strategic objectives and facilitate their success, FM should be a strategic function and the duty of making FM a strategic function rests on the shoulders of every FM practitioner.

It is you the FM practitioner that needs to work to align your FM functions with the core business of your organization so as to prove your strategic value. For

FM practitioners to be able to prove their strategic value, they need to, first of all, know the identity of FM and be convinced that it should be a strategic function.

FM Professional identity

With the dynamic change of the business environment, demand for FM grew and evolved rapidly. FM practitioners have to step up quickly and in order to keep pace with the wide and varied expectations. In the process of rapid growth, it is easy to get confused with what the FM professional identity truly is. As FM practitioners, if we are not sure of our identity, how do we communicate to others who we are, what we do and the values that this profession offers? Many FM practitioners are still stuck with the old FM identity as building maintenance; many others don't even know what the identity of FM is. If others do not know what we do, how do they know they can trust our professionalism for FM matters and call upon for

As FM practitioners, if we are not sure of our identity, how do we communicate to others who are, what we do and the values that this profession offers?

our ideas, advice or even opinion?

Let's test it out, say, you are asked; *"What do you do in FM?"* during an introduction. What will your answer be? Often, when I asked people similar question in the past, I received answers such as taking care of the building, attending to breakdowns, handling complaints from tenants or users or sometimes I even get answer such as "everything under the sun." This diversity of responses suggests the multidisciplinary nature of FM often challenges practitioners in being able to define their professional identity. It sure doesn't give the perception that FM is playing a very strategic role in the organization.

Why is it important to define the Professional Identity of FM?

It is the concept which describes how we perceive ourselves within our occupational context and how we communicate this to others. Our perception will affect our behaviour and self-confident. There was this practitioner who has been a property executive in his school for many years. Although his job title is only a property executive, he is responsible for all the facilities services in the school. After learning the importance of defining FM identity, he raised the awareness to the school board and in a short time, was promoted as FM Director. With the new designation, he represents his school with confident when dealing with his contractors as now they know that he is not only responsible for the duties, he also has the authority and power to make decision. His colleagues are also made aware that they have to involve and consult him when they have a need for support services. They do not bypass him and go straight to the principal of the school to request for the facilities and support services they required.

Why is it so difficult to define the Professional Identity of FM?

As we have already established in the earlier chapter, FM scope is non-core activities that support the core functions of the organization. However, non-core activities are wide and varied from organization to organization. For example, the scope of FM team in a commercial complex will defer greatly from an FM team that serves in a corporate office environment. Thus there is no shared sense of commonality amongst practitioners.

The task is made more complicated by the popularity of the trend of outsourcing and out-tasking the FM services to reduce operation expenses. It adds more confusion to the profession. As now, the non-core activities of the clients, have become the core function of the FM service providers. FM service providers primarily concern will be meeting the clients' requirements and expectations. Their concerns are unlikely to focus on enabling their clients' business operation success; rather they are concerned more about their profit and loss in providing the services to their clients. As such, the function tends to become tactical or operational instead of strategical.

With clarity, the top management is more willing to involve FM in their strategic planning as they understand that FM is there to facilitate the success of the operation through the provision of facilitate and support services.

So the task of defining FM identity is left to individual practitioner to their organization. For you to positively impact and influence management's view on FM functions, you need to able to communicate to them the FM identity. For instance, in view of the high rental of office space and expensive construction cost, senior management may be more willing to involve FM and discuss with them on maximizing space utilization before considering new acquisition or construction of the new space requirements.

Defining FM Identity.

What is FM responsible for? Simply, in a big picture, FM manages facilities and renders support services. What is the mission of FM (the purpose for managing facilities and delivering support services)? FM activities are focused on facilitating an organization's operations success. I hope these questions have helped you to define your FM identity in your organization.

FM activities are focused on facilitating an organization's operations success.

Now, for you to position FM functions as one that adds value to your organization, you need to be able to relate the above mission of FM to the senior management of your organization. FM must be able to market their services and create the awareness of their contributions to the organization.

Marketing your FM services. To start off, you need to ask yourself this question, *"what are the values that FM bring to the table that are different from the other functions within the organization?"* The answer you give to the question is going to differ according to your organization industry. The answer that someone in the hospitality industry gives is going to be different from the answer that someone in the IT industry gives. However, they should all going to border on the unique values that their services bring to the table.

Reflect on the types of FM activities that have significant impact on your organization's operations. Which FM services is crucial to your organization operations success? For a school, a safe and secure environment is critical. What have FM done to give the parents, the assurance that their child is safe at all times while they are within the school premises. Employees should be given the confident that every day, they are entering a safe, secure and conducive workplace.

With the above clarifications on the value of FM, you should be able to have positive thoughts and perception about the FM profession, and also see the profession in a positive light. Once your thoughts are clear about the identity of FM, you can be more certain and confident about the value of FM. And once you are more certain and sure about the value of FM, you can easily relate these values of FM to senior management and also change their views about your service.

Imagine that a new senior management staff was to ask you *"What do you do in FM?"* How may your answer affect how that recipient perceive you and FM? How will the new senior management staff recognize the value contribution of FM to the organization? Know that your answers about what you do in FM or What FM does will have an impact on the perception of the one who has asked the question.

Below are some samples of 2 to 3-liner answers that

may help you to formulate your own definition for your organization or your industry. If you give the below answers to the person asking you about FM services, there is no way that the person's views and perceptions about FM will not change.

> *"We keep the facilities operating at optimum performance to support the core business operations."*
>
> *"We ensure that the workplace is safe, secure and pleasant to enable a productive work environment."*
>
> *"We ensure that the facilities services are cost-effective solutions in serving the business operation's needs."*

Case for FM as a strategic function

FM has evolved over the years in keeping pace with the technological disruptions, the changing composition of the workforces, and new ways of business and working.

Years ago, the services of FM aren't so wide and varied. There are lesser automation, skyscrapers and specialize industrial complex. So, it is understandable that the management saw FM those days as an order taking function and they could not see the correlation between the execution of FM tasks and the growth and development of the organization.

Furthermore, senior management also perceived FM as a cost center those days – they believed that the FM was not adding directly to the profit of the organization yet, costs a lot of money to operate. Remember, we said earlier that apart from staff employment, facilities and its management is the second thing that costs organizations the most money. Most FM function do not practice chargeback and absorb all the expenditure under their function. Thus it gives management the perception that FM is a cost center and a necessary evil.

Also as FM services are wide and varied, combine with no clear professional identity, anything that others are not sure who to call, they will the FM team first. Now with the speed of interaction on social media spilling into the workplace, how can you expect a customer to wait on hold? No wonder every work order that comes in is marked as urgent or top priority. All these factors add on pressure and unnecessary the workload of an FM practitioner, and thus you can see why he is constantly fighting fire.

The constant firefighting gives off the perception to the management that FM is not performing well as supporting role. How then will they have time for strategic planning and involvement?

But as times continue to change, the workplace has also significantly evolved, and a lot of things has changed as well. Today, things are radically different, portable computer systems changed everything, and rapid improvements in technology also contributed to change a lot of things in the workplace. Office walls are removed as offices became open-plan. Due to the different changes in office arrangements, managers became their own secretaries, organizing their own meetings and getting their own coffees from machines. The board started to demand everything in an instant and employees have constant email access on mobile and tablets. The world has become digital, files are stored on server nodes, and the power needs of organizations has dramatically increased.

With all of these changes, the mission of FM has continued to evolve too. Generally, the mission of FM as we saw earlier was to operate in the background to ensure buildings and services operate safely and efficiently to allow people go about their duties effortlessly without having to worry about how the building functions. In the past, it was okay to see FM as a non-strategic function, but with the constant evolutions in the workplace and the attendant evolution of the skills needed to perform FM services in this age, there is a huge need for FM to be a strategic function.

Due to the above key shifts in workplaces as described, it is necessary that FM is positioned as a strategic function. The workplace has become more employee-centric, facilities have emerged as brand extensions, not to mention that facilities have become metrics to benchmark performance. Consequently, more skills and strategies are required to now manage facilities as opposed to what was obtainable in the past.

To better understand why FM should be position as a strategic function, we first look at how FM operations at a tactical level, as compared to if it is running at a strategic level.

Operating at a tactical level, FM will probably be receiving instructions and carrying out works as directed or instructed by a higher level or as told by other functions within the organization. Because they are not involved in the decision-making process of the organization, they were often out of synch with core happenings in the organization and not informed of the future plans of the organisation. As such, they may not know that the work request they received, may not solve or meet the stakeholders' needs. They are also not given a chance to propose alternatives.

For instance, a department may request for additional workstations to be set up as they are expanding. After the additional workstations have been set up, the department realized that it is not to their liking as all the usable space in the department are taken up, and now it has created a claustrophobic work environment, furthermore they also require additional meeting rooms to be set up. The new work request to FM would then be to relocate the additional workstations. This caused FM unnecessary rework and waste of time and resources. It also caused the organization not to be able to maximize their space utilization.

Besides, if FM is a tactical function, it means the FM team are likely not aware of the business environment and performance that the organization are facing, they are unlikely to be able to identify which FM services are crucial and critical to the organization. Thus, make resources allocation planning and decision making difficult. In turn, it will cause the organization also lose its flexibility and adaptability to the dynamic change of its environment. As mention in the earlier chapter, the speed of adaptability is crucial to the survival and success of the business.

That being said, if FM is positioned at a strategic level, how will the operations be like and how will FM at strategic level be able to better contribute value to its organization?

FM positioned at strategic level:

- ***Proactive:*** FM will be informed of the organization's long-term plans, planned goals, and organizational change, and will be involved in the meetings of senior management or board levels among directors. With the information they will get and the opportunity, FM can "be proactive" in proposing solution options for the needs for facilities in adapting to the change in the organization's operations or the addition of new facilities in accommodating new operations.

- ***Influence:*** FM is able to offer professional advice on the feasibilities for the acquisition, additions, and alterations of the workplace in supporting the organizational change.

- ***Value add:*** For instance, in the past, even till today, constant air volume (CAV) systems are used in buildings for air conditioning and ventilation. These types of air conditioning systems would incur higher amount of energy, thus increasing the electrical supply costs. Today, the use of variable air volume (VAV) systems and building automation enable better comfort air conditioning, yet incur lower energy. Being at the strategic level, it will give FM the opportunity to propose and introduce new technology to help organization maximize their operating expenses in the long term rather than to base the procurement decision on the initial price.

We have established above that when FM function is operating as a strategic function, it will achieve its optimum potential and valuable contributions to organization. However, the fact remains that not all FM functions are given that opportunity in their organization. Nonetheless, our professionalism would require us to continue to pursue the FM's mission – that is to facilitate business operations success; focusing on the

When FM function is operating as a strategic function, it will achieve its optimum potential and valuable contributions to organization.

effectiveness and efficiency of the organization's operations.

Now let's look at how can FM activities can be planned to align and support the organization's strategic objectives. Below illustrates an overview of how the FM function should be structured in supporting its organization's strategic objectives.

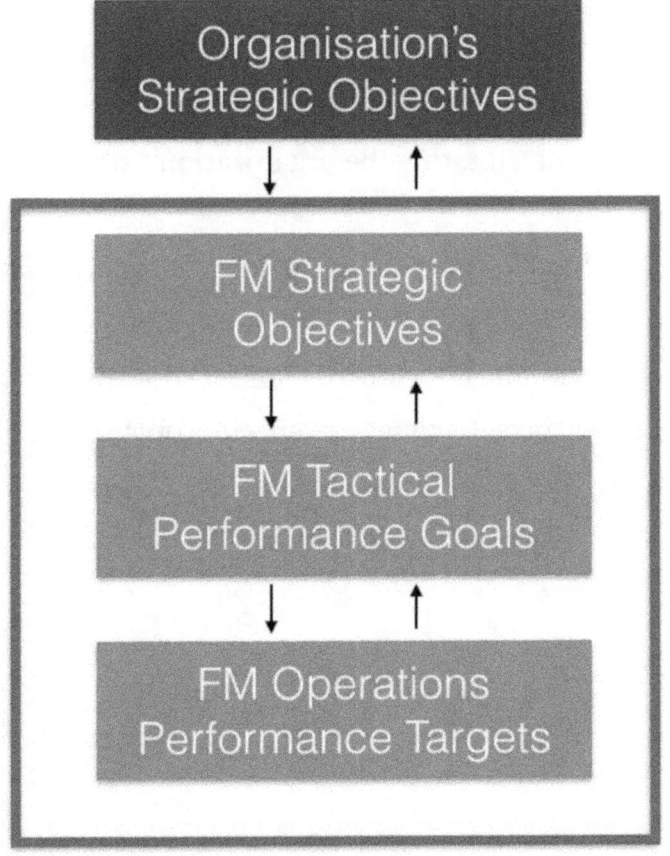

The above illustration shows a clear structure on how the FM performance, services, and activities can be aligned to support the achievement of the organization's strategic objectives.

Let me explain starting with the cascading of the organization's strategic objectives to FM strategic objectives.

The FM strategic objectives are translated from the organization's strategies and their need for facilities services in facilitating the organization's operations.

Within the FM function, its strategies are translated into goals at the tactical level, to plan, organize, direct, monitor, control and coordinate the resources in achieving the specific objectives. The goals will then be translated into Key Performance Levels, as Targets for the operations.

3

WHY FM IS NOT A COST CENTRE

In the previous chapters, we mentioned that management have often perceived FM as:

- An order taking function
- Support role
- Cost centre
- A non-strategic function

We have been able to make a case for why FM is a strategic function. Next, we want to talk about why FM is not a cost centre. First, what is a cost centre? A cost centre only incurs costs (expenses) but does not generate revenue. There is a wide perception by management that FM is only a cost centre, and due to that perception, many times, FM practitioners' proposal for capital improvements are turned down, and FM services are not able to keep pace with technology. That's why to better support the organization with its operations; we need to change their perception of FM being a cost centre - draining away the resources of the organization.

So, why is FM not a cost center?

FM spends to retain organizations' wealth, so it is not a cost center. A function is only a cost centre if it only incurs cost without adding value to the organization. However, this is not the case for FM. Yes, FM spends money but the purpose is to help the organization achieve operations success, which means that the money is spent to retain the organization's wealth. To further understand how FM is not a cost center, let's do quick learning on Finance. Let's see what the formula for profit is. You'll probably remember that profit is simply revenue minus expenses.

> *FM spends money but the purpose is to help the organization achieve operations success, which means that the money is spent to retain the organization's*

Look at the illustration below:

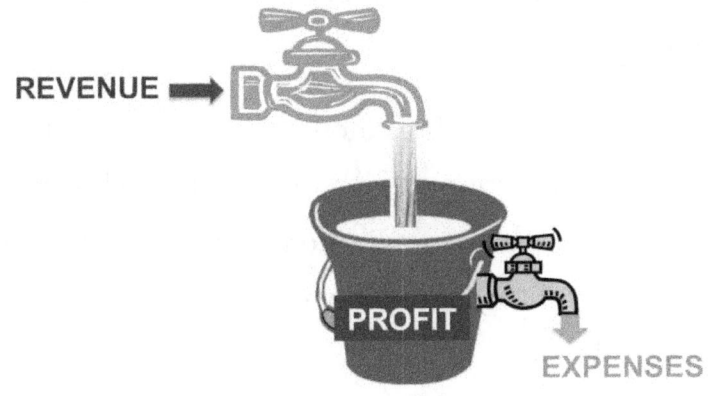

In the above illustration, the "Revenue" of the organization is represented by the bigger inflow tap at the top whereas the "Expenses" is represented by the outflow, from the smaller tap. The water retained in the pail is the "Profit."

FM may retain the organisation's wealth through preventing profit leakages and contribute to its organization's profit by reducing the operating expenses.

This illustration is intended to allow FM to have an overview under-standing of where FM may retain the organisation's wealth through preventing profit leakages and contribute to its organization's profit by reducing the operating expenses.

What may be the potential causes for the profit leakages?

- System breakdown – operations interruption and loss of production hours
- Non legal complication – lawsuits, fine and some-times shutdown
- Work Accidents – lawsuits and compensations.

The above mentioned profit leak-ages are actually avoidable. These are the cause for **FM expenditure**. FM spends on preventive measures and maintenance. Preventive maintenance pro-grammes are set up to ensure that operations can continue smoothly with minimum down-time. Extra measures are put in place to make sure that the organization meets the various legal requirements. Extras are spent on making sure

FM expenditure are towards preventing those avoidable loses, to extend the useful life of the equipment in the organization and to ensure that the operations are in compliance with the legal requirements.

the office workstations are ergonomic and safe. Preventive measures are put in place to reduce incident of slip, trip, and fall.

FM expenditure are towards preventing those avoidable loses, to extend the useful life of the equipment in the organization and to ensure that the operations are in compliance with the legal requirements. When the facilities are working optimally, the organization records low downtime and production is increased. Also, when the organization's facilities are maintained to meet the various legal requirements and regulations, the organizations won't have to pay huge sums in form of fines for non-compliance with regulations and legal requirements.

Another avenue of FM expenditure is on initiatives that reduce the operating expenses. For instance, installing motion sensor to control lighting, recycling of condensate water and installing façade to help cool the building. These are some of the initiatives that FM can help to implement and reduce the operating cost.

With the above illustration and explanation, it is clear to see that FM is not a cost centre, for it spends money to help the organization retain its wealth. Why are we spending a lot of time to talk about why FM is not a cost centre? It is to help you to be in a better position to relate to senior management why they should not overlook FM request for funds and trust FM professionalism.

Worth of FM value contributions

In this section, we want to talk about the *"worth of FM value contribution."* Hopefully, you have begun to understand the need for FM to be equipped with some knowledge on the essentials of finance so that FM can better relate to its senior management on how FM indeed is a value-adding business resource.

> *FM needs to communicate in finance and business language to help the senior management to better appreciate the works of FM in relation to how FM can add value to the organization.*

In order to relate that, FM needs to communicate in finance and business language to help the senior management to better appreciate the works of FM in relation to how FM can add value to the organization. It is no news to you and me that FM is often labelled as a cost-centre, the money spending department, the department which causes lowering of the year-end-bonus, and other neg-ative names.

Now, you're going to learn how to communicate these FM values to your senior management so that they can appreciate and understand.

Let me share the formula I usually use when presenting my team's improvements initiative that will contribute to 5% reduction in the FM operations budget to impress the senior management.

Example, FM achieved a 5% reduction in its $10 million operating budget, which amounts to $500,000. If the organization's sales are marked up by 10% over its cost, what would the FM savings of $500,000 be equivalent to in sales? That would be $5 million sales.

Impressive work of FM isn't it? I did that to impress upon the senior management of FM's value-adding potentials in equivalence to the core business functions. Do you think the senior management was impressed? Yes, they were, and the CEO rewarded the team recognizing the team's valuable contribution to the organization.

The bottom line is that it is important that we know the value of our services and recognize the worth of the FM function. Be confident to articulate our value contribution in finance and business language, do not confuse them with the technical terms or drawings unless your senior management are keen to know more on the engineering aspects.

FM as a business advantage to organizations

In this section, we want to quickly look at the different ways that FM can deliver competitive advantage to organizations.

Here are my three principal justifications.

1. FM can add advantage to its organizations by *"Increasing workplace effectiveness and efficiency"* such as through designing and locating the departments' workplace that promotes collaborations and productivity. When

there is improved collaboration and productivity in the workplace, the organization's profit will definitely shoot up, an advantage to the organization.

2. FM can add advantage to its organization by *"Initiating innovation that improves facilities services in enhancing business operations,"* such as initiating Integrated Workplace Management System to enable real-time feedback or request for FM services.

3. FM can add advantage to organizations through *"Implementing continual improvements in facilities operations and workplace quality"* such as healthy indoor air quality level, safe use of facilities, and so on and so forth. These are just some of my justifications, and you will want to think and write down a couple more other reasons that suit your organization.

In ending this chapter, we have to note that it is important that we know the value of our services and recognize the worth of FM functions. As said earlier, if we do not define ourselves, others will define us. Not to mention that we if we don't define ourselves, we will find it difficult to position our services to the senior management in our organizations as a value adding-adding centre rather than a cost centre.

4

GETTING STARTED

In the previous chapters, we have succeeded in defining FM, its key responsibilities and mission. We have also made a case for why FM should be a strategic function, as well seen why FM is a value centre rather than a cost centre or profit centre. In this chapter, we want to see the various steps of practicing FM the right way.

If you practice FM the right way, you will position your role to the senior management as a strategic function, and you will also position your function as a value center instead of a cost center. Let's get started.

1. Conduct facilities condition survey

The purpose of conducting facilities condition survey is to identify performance gaps, and to carry out corrective actions.

As facilities represent a significant proportion of investments in building, they are valuable assets to organizations. Facilities deteriorate with time and use affecting the operation performance. It is the primary responsibility of facilities management to ensure that the condition of facilities is maintained and improved. Deterioration of the condition of facilities can also lead to undesirable outcomes like business disruptions, occupational health hazards, operational wastage and asset depreciation.

Facilities Condition Survey is a systematic process to examine the facilities services systems and their components. The purpose is to assess, report and advise on the state of the facilities. It is akin to taking stock of the facilities to provide basic information for the efficient facilities management. Regular exercises and formal reports of condition surveys would provide the platform for laying down long and short-term facilities plans. The long-term plans would serve the business strategy while the short-term plans would support the business operations.

Facilities Condition Survey methods range from simple inspection done visually to detailed assessment using auditory and kinesthetic sensory acuities or engaging external professionals to conduct even more detailed investigations and examinations. The scope is such as:

- external examination of building;
- evaluation of the facilities performance;
- evaluation of the operations within facilities;
- compliance with legal, safety and health requirements; and
- Identify future facilities requirements.

The essence of conducting the facilities survey is to know the conditions of the buildings or facilities under your care, together with the condition of all equipment. The survey is to provide a good head start on where to get started on where and what needs the most attention. It's a good start to take stock of all the facilities – form an asset register, if you do not know what you have, how are you going to manage it.

Finding No.	Location	Areas for Improvement	Photograph/Operation Report	Corrective Action Priority	Proposed Corrective Action	Estimated Costs	Planned Schedule	Approver (sign)
1-1	B3-L1-1-E	To replace corroded drain pan		1	To replace 2 ft condenser drain pan during the next maintenance	\$5300 per drain pan Total: \$5600	1st week June	
1-2	B3-L1-1-W	Worn Condenser fins are brittle and damaged		2	To replace 2 ft condenser unit	\$3000/CU Total: \$6000	3rd week June	
2-1	B2-R-W	Worn cooling tower, infills are collapsing		1	To refurbish the cooling tower	\$5000	End May during production break	

Conducting the facilities survey an essential skill for FM practitioners. Hence, for you to be proactive in sustaining the intended performance of the facilities, you need to know how to conduct a survey of the facilities in your care.

2. Set performance targets

The aim of setting performance targets is to help you have an overview of the FM activities you should focus on and how you should set the FM activities performance targets so that you can identify and direct the FM activities that support the organization's strategic objectives.

The table on the next page shows a common scorecard used by most senior management, known as Balanced Scorecard. The scorecard was developed and made popular by Dr. Robert Kaplan and Dr. David Norton. I strongly encourage you to get hold of the book to understand better. Most organizations adopt the four key areas of business strategy as shown on the card: Customer, Internal Processes, Financial and Learning & Growth.

Organisation's Objectives	Facilities Operations Measurement Areas	Measurement
CUSTOMER What do occupants and users of facilities value from facilities operations?	Comfort, security and safety of workplace environment	Survey of customer satisfaction
	Customer care	Interview regarding customers' experiences
INTERNAL PROCESSES What processes must facilities operations align with the business processes?	Promotion of workplace productivity	Satisfaction with workplace quality and service standards
	Space usage	Space optimisation
FINANCIAL How are facilities operations managed in terms of value for money?	Value for money	Efficiency of utilities consumption
	Within budget	Variance between planned and actual expenditure. See Figure 5.14 for an example of a Variance Report
LEARNING and GROWTH How may facilities staff maintain or improve to support the organisation?	Keep pace with advancement in facilities practices and technology	Attendance of training on new legal compliance or code of practice
	Contribute value to organisation	Ability to improve facilities and services

Here is how FM may adapt its activities to align with the organization's objectives. Let's look at the table. There are three columns. On the right is the organization's objectives, which lists the four key areas of business strategy, the Facilities Operations Measurement Area and the Measurement.

Let's look at the organization's Objectives' column first. Here, I have provided questions to help guide you to understand what is expected of FM for each of the strategic areas. The Facilities Operations Measurement Areas are the outcome of FM performance in supporting each of the strategic areas. The Measurement indicates the means of measuring the performance of the respective service deliveries.

The cascading of the organization's strategic objectives to FM activities performance targets will help you to decide what activities that are important to focus on and to clearly understand how FM activities are aligned to support the organization's performance.

It is expected that you set your department's performance targets every year and also to transmit same to the senior management of your organization.

3. Involve your functions with other departments within the organization

This is one surefire way to increase the satisfaction of other department heads with your services. It doesn't always have to be with the senior management, simply meeting with other department heads to know areas where your services can help them deliver their core functions more efficiently can help raise your strategic position in your organization.

Often, different departments have unique service requirements and needs that FM needs to know of and attend to. Now, how are you going to know about these special requirements if you don't meet with the heads of these departments occasionally? When you understand the needs of the various departments and put efforts to run an all-inclusive service delivery, these departments would appreciate your effort in facilitating their operations and will be more cooperative and accommodating. This will create a synergy that is vital to any organization success.

The needs of some departments may often be different from that of the general organization, and you can periodically schedule meetings with them to craft a kind of informal service level agreement. Make it FM responsible to make it easier for them to perform their job. This will also keep you abreast with the operation's needs. Apart from raising the perceptions of these different departments about your functions, including meetings with these various departments in your reports to the senior management will reinforcement your mission to them – FM facilitate operations success!

4. Make your FM department accountable to senior management by providing reports

Often, FM practitioners don't give reports on their activities to senior management of their organizations. Hence, they don't see the FM efforts and contributions. It is not just enough to do an excellent job for your organization, but it is also important that you provide high-level reporting to the senior management taking into account all your measurements of performance during the year and also summarize your accomplishments for the year.

Preparing this weekly, monthly or yearly reports can be time-consuming. However, it is important to show the senior management the impact that your department is making in the organization. This is one way to change their misperception of your department as just a cost center. Remember that the other departments in your organization often tender daily, weekly, monthly, and yearly reports detailing their achievement, so, you too should do same.

In your report, always cover your accomplishments as a department, performance to key performance indicators, projects that need to be executed, and also issues that need to be addressed in the department, not forgetting to include budget and how it was used for your various activities.

As mention earlier, when you provide these details, you are being proactive and position your department as an active contributor to the organisation success.

The report, whether annual, weekly or daily, should contain all the activities accomplished within the said period. The report may contain such topics such as health and safety accomplishments, key performance indicator performance results, energy management accomplishments, landscaping services, maintenance operations accomplishments, a depiction of the goals and objective that are in alignment with the organization's goals and objectives.

The presentation of the report matters a lot; presenting a plain document might not add appeal to it. Preferably, use pictures, graphs, charts to illustrate what you are trying to portray. A report that is well written and presented shows the senior management the things happening in your department, which is a good way to steer away from the perception of being a cost centre. Even though the senior management might just want to narrow to the areas of their interest, providing a comprehensive report is a sign that your department is doing a great job and boosts the morale of your department.

5. Provide extra services that are recognized and valued by your organization

The function of FM permeates the entire organization, and there are always ways you can build relationship across the organization. There are several areas where you can provide extra services recognized and valued by your organization. These include the following:

- You could decide to get involved in emergency response
- You could get involved in disaster recovery management
- You could get involved in interfacing with the real estate acquisition and leasing process, etc.

The above and more are all activities that can significantly improve the senior management's perception of your department and its function. With an enhanced perception of your functions, your professionalism will be respected and your expert opinion will be sought.

You and every member of your FM team should endeavour to join cross-functional teams and committees to integrate the functions of FM within every nook and cranny of your organization. As you continue to make efforts to provide extra valued and recognized services within your organization, senior management taking note of your efforts, will trust your FM mission and recognize that FM add a business advantage to their organisation.

6. Seek to improve your organization using quality techniques and that are recognized in your industry

Across different industries and professions, professional recognition and awards help to elevate the status of practitioners. Same is also obtainable in the FM industry. Getting recognition and awards from recognized bodies and organizations such as APPA, BOMA, IFMA, etc. can help to enhance your organisation branding and status. In turn, we can demonstrate that FM can contribute values to your organization.

There are many ways you could get recognition for your organisation by some of these bodies. Example, if you participate in competition occasionally organized by these bodies, or achieve awards such as "Green Building," "Barrier Free Access," etc., your organization could get featured in the news or journals. It will improve the perception of customers towards your organization and gain brand loyalty.

By implementing the above suggestions, you will be living out the FM mission – demonstrate that FM is here to facilitate operations success. Your organization will then realize that FM is an added business advantage.

CONCLUSION

For many years, senior management have viewed FM as a support role, a cost centre, an order taking and non-strategic function. As a result of these perceptions, FM practitioners continued to be out of synch with the core business strategy of their organizations, isolated from management meetings, and were also unable to advance their role as strategic partners in their various organizations.

We noted that the composition of the workplace in the past contributed to the above perceptions of FM described above. But as the workplace has continued to evolve over the years, FM, on the other hand, has also continued to expand and evolve its services and values to the organization. With Digital Revolution, the advancement of technology from analog electronic and mechanical devices to the digital technology available today and the emergence of workplaces as open plan areas, the demand for FM services has changed drastically. Because of these many changes in the workplace, senior management are beginning to realize the value and professionalism of FM practitioners.

Now, it is for the FM practitioners to step up, be confident and proactive in the partnerships of management in their organizations. To create this strategic partnership, FM practitioners need

- to understand and be committed to the mission of FM
- to uphold the professional identity of FM,
- to be proactive in improving your organisation flexibility and adaptability in their business environment.

I wish you success in embarking this FM journey. Know that you are not alone, join the FM community and be linked with other fellow practitioners. Let's us support one another and raise up the standard and professionalism of this practice.

RESOURCES

Steven Ee has written a number of articles on facilities management which were published in *The Straits Times*. Further reading on value-add strategies for your facilities management practice, download the articles from www.fms-1.com/media, under "Publications". He regularly contributes "Quotes on FM" and articles on FM on through *LinkedIn* where he focuses on how FM practitioners can deliver competitive advantage to organisations.

He also runs FMS Associates Asia, which was founded in 2007 with a mission to increase the recognition of the FM profession as a value-adding function and business advantage to organisations. FMS Associates Asia offers a series of courses to equip FM practitioners with skills to enhance their own performance as well as their organisations'.

🅢 Steven Ee

Website: www.stevenee.com
email: steven@stevenee.com

REERENCES

Cotts, D., Roper, K.O., & Payant, R.P., 2009, The Facility Management Handbook, 3rd edn., Amacom, USA.

Ee, S., 2015, Value-Based Facilities Management – How Facilities Practitioners Can Deliver Competitive Advantage to Organisations, Candid Creation, Singapore.

FMS Associates Asia, 2015, Overseeing Facilities Operations, Singapore.

FMS Associates Asia, 2015, Establishing Facilities Essentials, Singapore.

TPC Training System, 1981, Implementing a Preventive Maintenance Program, Technical Publishing, USA.

www.ingramcontent.com/pod-product-compliance
Lightning Source LLC
Chambersburg PA
CBHW070216230526
45471CB00002B/964